THE ORIGINAL INDESTRUCTIBLES

For ages 0 and up!

Books babies can really sink their gums into!

Wind blows. Hang on to your hat!
Snow falls. Nose so cold!
Sun shines. The world is smiling!

Discover all the weather with
a book that's INDESTRUCTIBLE.

DEAR PARENTS: High-Color, High-Contrast INDESTRUCTIBLES nurture your baby's developing eyesight. And they're built for the way babies "read": with their hands and mouths. Indestructibles won't rip or tear and are 100% washable. They're made for baby to hold, grab, chew, pull, and bend. *CHEW ALL THESE AND MORE!*

$5.99 US / $8.99 Can.
ISBN 978-1-5235-1946-0

Copyright © 2023 by Indestructibles, LLC. Used under license. Illustrations copyright © 2023 by Workman Publishing Co., Inc.

All rights reserved. Library of Congress Cataloging-in-Publication Data is available. WORKMAN is a registered trademark of Workman Publishing Co., Inc., a subsidiary of Hachette Book Group, Inc.

Distributed in the United Kingdom by Hachette Book Group, UK, Carmelite House, 50 Victoria Embankment, London EC4Y 0DZ. Distributed in Europe by Hachette Livre, 58 rue Jean Bleuzen, 92 178 Vanves Cedex, France.

Contact special.markets@hbgusa.com regarding special discounts for bulk purchases.

All INDESTRUCTIBLES books have been safety-tested and meet or exceed ASTM-F963 and CPSIA guidelines. INDESTRUCTIBLES is a registered trademark of Indestructibles, LLC.

Cover © 2023 Hachette Book Group, Inc. First printing April 2023 I 10 9 8 7 6 5 4 3 2 1
Printed in China

WORKMAN PUBLISHING CO., INC. 1290 Avenue of the Americas, New York, NY 10104 • indestructiblesinc.com